It's Autumn!

Acknowledgments

Executive Editor: Diane Sharpe
Supervising Editor: Stephanie Muller
Design Manager: Sharon Golden
Page Design: Simon Balley Design Associates
Photography: Bruce Coleman: cover (middle right), pages 9, 19, 23, 27;
Garden Picture Library: pages 15, 17; Image Bank: page 13; Tony Stone:
cover (top right), page 21; ZEFA: page 11.

ISBN 0-8114-3706-X

It's Autumn!

Michael Herschell

Illustrated by

Shirley Tourret

STECK-VAUGHN
COMPANY
ELEMENTARY • SECONDARY • ADULT • LIBRARY

4

It is often misty on autumn mornings. It is also cooler outside in the autumn.

7

In the autumn, the leaves on many trees turn yellow, orange, brown, and red.

I like playing
in the leaves.

There are many leaves
on the ground, too.

10

In the autumn, the leaves fall off many trees. That is why the autumn is also called the fall.

Sometimes the autumn wind is very strong. The wind blows the leaves off trees.

This kind of tree is called an evergreen because it stays green all year. Evergreens often have needles instead of leaves.

Sometimes people in the country
have bonfires.

Those are called rose hips. They are the fruit of the rose bush.

20

Apples and pears get ripe in
the autumn.

Look at all the birds sitting in a row.

Those are swallows. They're getting ready to fly away.

22

In the autumn, many birds migrate
to warmer places. They stay there
for the winter.

In the autumn, farmers store hay
for their animals.

In the winter, the animals will need
to eat the hay.

In the autumn, squirrels store acorns
to eat during the winter.

In the autumn, it gets dark earlier in the evening.

These are some things we might see in the autumn. Can you name them?

Index